The Hagopian Institute, LLC has compiled the _Quote Junkie_ series. The overall series includes over 8,000 quotes, focusing mostly on short quotes that can be used in everyday life as sources of wisdom and inspiration. This particular edition of the series includes funny, inspirational, and political quotes from some of the United State's greatest presidents. Please enjoy this edition of the series, and share these quotes with your coworkers, friends, and family.

Todd Hagopian

President

The Hagopian Institute, LLC

Everybody likes a compliment.

Abraham Lincoln

Books serve to show a man that those original thoughts of his aren't very new at all.

Abraham Lincoln

Give me six hours to chop down a tree and I will spend the first four sharpening the axe.

Abraham Lincoln

I will prepare and some day my chance will come.

Abraham Lincoln

Some single mind must be master, else there will be no agreement in anything.

Abraham Lincoln

Things may come to those who wait, but only the things left by those who hustle.

Abraham Lincoln

When I do good, I feel good. When I do bad, I feel bad. That's my religion.

Abraham Lincoln

Am I not destroying my enemies when I make friends of them?

Abraham Lincoln

Don't worry when you are not recognized, but strive to be worthy of recognition

Abraham Lincoln

I never had a policy; I have just tried to do my very best each and every day.

Abraham Lincoln

I walk slowly, but I never walk backward.

Abraham Lincoln

My great concern is not whether you have failed, but whether you are content with your failure.

Abraham Lincoln

I do not think much of a man who is not wiser today than he was yesterday

Abraham Lincoln

The things I want to know are in books; my best friend is the man who'll get me a book I ain't read.

Abraham Lincoln

And in the end it's not the years in your life that count. It's the life in your years.

Abraham Lincoln

Be sure you put your feet in the right place, then stand firm.

Abraham Lincoln

He has a right to criticize, who has a heart to help.

Abraham Lincoln

I don't like that man. I must get to know him better.

Abraham Lincoln

Most folks are about as happy as they make their minds up to be.

Abraham Lincoln

No man has a good enough memory to be a successful liar.

Abraham Lincoln

*Stand with anybody that stands right, stand with him while he is right and
part with him when he goes wrong.*

Abraham Lincoln

Tact is the ability to describe others as they see themselves.

Abraham Lincoln

The best thing about the future is that it comes one day at a time.

Abraham Lincoln

To sin by silence when they should protest makes cowards of men.

Abraham Lincoln

We should be too big to take offense and too noble to give it.

Abraham Lincoln

Whatever you are, be a good one.

Abraham Lincoln

You cannot escape the responsibility of tomorrow by evading it today.

Abraham Lincoln

The ballot is stronger than the bullet.

Abraham Lincoln

A house divided against itself cannot stand.

Abraham Lincoln

Allow the president to invade a neighboring nation, whenever he shall deem it necessary to repel an invasion, and you allow him to do so whenever he may choose to say he deems it necessary for such a purpose - and you allow him to make war at pleasure

Abraham Lincoln

America will never be destroyed from the outside. If we falter and lose our freedoms, it will be because we destroyed ourselves.

Abraham Lincoln

Ballots are the rightful and peaceful successors to bullets.

Abraham Lincoln

I can make more generals, but horses cost money.

Abraham Lincoln

A friend is one who has the same enemies as you have.

Abraham Lincoln

A woman is the only thing I am afraid of that I know will not hurt me.

Abraham Lincoln

All I am, or can be, I owe to my angel mother.

Abraham Lincoln

Better to remain silent and be thought a fool than to speak out and remove all doubt.

Abraham Lincoln

Common looking people are the best in the world: that is the reason the Lord makes so many of them.

Abraham Lincoln

Every one desires to live long, but no one would be old.

Abraham Lincoln

Government of the people, by the people, for the people, shall not perish from the Earth.

Abraham Lincoln

How many legs does a dog have if you call the tail a leg? Four. Calling a tail a leg doesn't make it a leg.

Abraham Lincoln

I have always found that mercy bears richer fruits than strict justice.

Abraham Lincoln

I remember my mother's prayers and they have always followed me. They have clung to me all my life.

Abraham Lincoln

If I were two-faced, would I be wearing this one?

Abraham Lincoln

If this is coffee, please bring me some tea; but if this is tea, please bring me some coffee.

Abraham Lincoln

Let not him who is houseless pull down the house of another, but let him work diligently and build one for himself, thus by example assuring that his own shall be safe from violence when built.

Abraham Lincoln

Marriage is neither heaven nor hell, it is simply purgatory.

Abraham Lincoln

Nearly all men can stand adversity, but if you want to test a man's character, give him power.

Abraham Lincoln

Never stir up litigation. A worse man can scarcely be found than one who does this.

Abraham Lincoln

No matter how much cats fight, there always seem to be plenty of kittens.

Abraham Lincoln

Public opinion in this country is everything.

Abraham Lincoln

The best way to get a bad law repealed is to enforce it strictly.

Abraham Lincoln

The time comes upon every public man when it is best for him to keep his lips closed.

Abraham Lincoln

These capitalists generally act harmoniously and in concert, to fleece the people

Abraham Lincoln

Those who deny freedom to others deserve it not for themselves.

Abraham Lincoln

What kills a skunk is the publicity it gives itself.

Abraham Lincoln

When you have got an elephant by the hind legs and he is trying to run away, it's best to let him run.

Abraham Lincoln

Whenever I hear anyone arguing for slavery, I feel a strong impulse to see it tried on him personally.

Abraham Lincoln

You have to do your own growing no matter how tall your grandfather was.

Abraham Lincoln

Any man worth his salt will stick up for what he believes right, but it takes a slightly better man to acknowledge instantly and without reservation that he is in error.

Andrew Jackson

Americans are not a perfect people, but we are called to a perfect mission.

Andrew Jackson

As long as our government is administered for the good of the people, and is regulated by their will; as long as it secures to us the rights of persons and of property, liberty of conscience and of the press, it will be worth defending.

Andrew Jackson

The brave man inattentive to his duty, is worth little more to his country than the coward who deserts in the hour of danger.

Andrew Jackson

If the Union is once severed, the line of separation will grow wider and wider, and the controversies which are now debated and settled in the halls of legislation will then be tried in fields of battle and determined by the sword.

Andrew Jackson

No one need think that the world can be ruled without blood. The civil sword shall and must be red and bloody.

Andrew Jackson

Nullification means insurrection and war; and the other states have a right to put it down.

Andrew Jackson

Peace, above all things, is to be desired, but blood must sometimes be spilled to obtain it on equable and lasting terms.

Andrew Jackson

To the victors belong the spoils.

Andrew Jackson

War is a blessing compared with national degradation.

Andrew Jackson

All the rights secured to the citizens under the Constitution are worth nothing, and a mere bubble, except guaranteed to them by an independent and virtuous Judiciary.

Andrew Jackson

Democracy shows not only its power in reforming governments, but in regenerating a race of men and this is the greatest blessing of free governments.

Andrew Jackson

Disunion by force is treason.

Andrew Jackson

Fear not, the people may be deluded for a moment, but cannot be corrupted.

Andrew Jackson

I am a Senator against my wishes and feelings, which I regret more than any other of my life.

Andrew Jackson

I would sincerely regret, and which never shall happen whilst I am in office, a military guard around the President.

Andrew Jackson

It is a damn poor mind indeed which can't think of at least two ways to spell any word.

Andrew Jackson

It is to be regretted that the rich and powerful too often bend the acts of government to their own selfish purposes.

Andrew Jackson

One man with courage makes a majority

Andrew Jackson

Take time to deliberate; but when the time for action arrives, stop thinking and go in.

Andrew Jackson

The Bible is the rock on which this Republic rests.

Andrew Jackson

The wisdom of man never yet contrived a system of taxation that would operate with perfect equality.

Andrew Jackson

There is no pleasure in having nothing to do; the fun is having lots to do and not doing it.

Andrew Jackson

If I am shot at, I want no man to be in the way of the bullet.

Andrew Johnson

Honest conviction is my courage; the Constitution is my guide.

Andrew Johnson

I am sworn to uphold the Constitution as Andy Johnson understands it and interprets it.

Andrew Johnson

I feel incompetent to perform duties... which have been so unexpectedly thrown upon me.

Andrew Johnson

If the rabble were lopped off at one end and the aristocrats at the other, all would be well with the country.

Andrew Johnson

The goal to strive for is a poor government but a rich people.

Andrew Johnson

They don't remember a time when we had to drink from a different water fountain. We can't go back. We can never go back.

Andrew Johnson

The bud of victory is always in the truth.

Benjamin Harrison

Great lives never go out; they go on.

Benjamin Harrison

I knew that my staying up would not change the election result if I were defeated, while if elected I had a hard day ahead of me. So I thought a night's rest was best in any event.

Benjamin Harrison

I pity the man who wants a coat so cheap that the man or woman who produces the cloth will starve in the process.

Benjamin Harrison

We Americans have no commission from God to police the world.

Benjamin Harrison

When and under what conditions is the black man to have a free ballot? When is he in fact to have those full civil rights which have so long been his in law?

Benjamin Harrison

Nothing in the world can take the place of Persistence. Talent will not; nothing is more common than unsuccessful men with talent. Genius will not; unrewarded genius is almost a proverb. Education will not; the world is full of educated derelicts. Persistence and determination alone are omnipotent. The slogan 'Press On' has solved and always will solve the problems of the human race.

Calvin Coolidge

Don't expect to build up the weak by pulling down the strong.

Calvin Coolidge

Industry, thrift and self-control are not sought because they create wealth, but because they create character.

Calvin Coolidge

It takes a great man to be a good listener.

Calvin Coolidge

Little progress can be made by merely attempting to repress what is evil. Our great hope lies in developing what is good.

Calvin Coolidge

We cannot do everything at once, but we can do something at once.

Calvin Coolidge

No enterprise can exist for itself alone. It ministers to some great need, it performs some great service, not for itself, but for others; or failing therein, it ceases to be profitable and ceases to exist.

Calvin Coolidge

No man ever listened himself out of a job.

Calvin Coolidge

Economy is the method by which we prepare today to afford the improvements of tomorrow.

Calvin Coolidge

If I had permitted my failures, or what seemed to me at the time a lack of success, to discourage me I cannot see any way in which I would ever have made progress.

Calvin Coolidge

No person was ever honored for what he received. Honor has been the reward for what he gave.

Calvin Coolidge

Those who trust to chance must abide by the results of chance.

Calvin Coolidge

I have never been hurt by what I have not said.

Calvin Coolidge

If you see ten troubles coming down the road, you can be sure that nine will run into the ditch before they reach you.

Calvin Coolidge

Heroism is not only in the man, but in the occasion.

Calvin Coolidge

There is no dignity quite so impressive, and no one independence quite so important, as living within your means.

Calvin Coolidge

Knowledge comes, but wisdom lingers.

Calvin Coolidge

Perhaps one of the most important accomplishments of my administration has been minding my own business.

Calvin Coolidge

If you don't say anything, you won't be called on to repeat it.

Calvin Coolidge

Collecting more taxes than is absolutely necessary is legalized robbery.

Calvin Coolidge

Prosperity is only an instrument to be used, not a deity to be worshipped.

Calvin Coolidge

Men may die, but the fabric of our free institutions remains unshaken.

Chester Arthur

The extravagant expenditure of public money is an evil not to be measured by the value of that money to the people who are taxed for it.

Chester Arthur

I may be president of the United States, but my private life is nobody's damned business.

Chester Arthur

Since I came here I have learned that Chester A. Arthur is one man and the President of the United States is another.

Chester Arthur

A Republic without parties is a complete anomaly. The histories of all popular governments show absurd is the idea of their attempting to exist without parties.

Franklin Pierce

Frequently the more trifling the subject, the more animated and protracted the discussion.

Franklin Pierce

If we are wise, let us prepare for the worst.

George Washington

Let your Discourse with Men of Business be Short and Comprehensive

George Washington

Labor to keep alive in your breast that little spark of celestial fire, called conscience.

George Washington

Associate with men of good quality if you esteem your own reputation; for it is better to be alone than in bad company.

George Washington

If the freedom of speech is taken away then dumb and silent we may be led, like sheep to the slaughter.

George Washington

Liberty, when it begins to take root, is a plant of rapid growth.

George Washington

Arbitrary power is most easily established on the ruins of liberty abused to licentiousness

George Washington

Firearms are second only to the Constitution in importance; they are the peoples' liberty's teeth.

George Washington

Guard against the impostures of pretended patriotism.

George Washington

Happiness and moral duty are inseparably connected.

George Washington

It is impossible to rightly govern a nation without God and the Bible.

George Washington

The Constitution is the guide which I never will abandon.

George Washington

My first wish is to see this plague of mankind, war, banished from the earth.

George Washington

To be prepared for war is one of the most effective means of preserving peace.

George Washington

War - An act of violence whose object is to constrain the enemy, to accomplish our will.

George Washington

Be courteous to all, but intimate with few, and let those few be well tried before you give them your confidence.

George Washington

Happiness and moral duty are inseparably connected.

George Washington

It is better to offer no excuse than a bad one.

George Washington

Worry is the interest paid by those who borrow trouble.

George Washington

Few men have virtue to withstand the highest bidder.

George Washington

To err is natural; to rectify error is glory.

George Washington

There is but one straight course, and that is to seek truth and pursue it steadily.

George Washington

Someday, following the example of the United States of America, there will be a United States of Europe.

George Washington

The foolish and wicked practice of profane cursing and swearing is a vice so mean and low that every person of sense and character detests and despises it.

George Washington

Worry is the interest paid by those who borrow trouble.

George Washington

A government for the people must depend for its success on the intelligence, the morality, the justice, and the interest of the people themselves.

Grover Cleveland

A truly American sentiment recognizes the dignity of labor and the fact that honor lies in honest toil.

Grover Cleveland

In the scheme of our national government, the presidency is preeminently the people's office.

Grover Cleveland

Public officers are the servants and agents of the people, to execute the laws which the people have made.

Grover Cleveland

Communism is a hateful thing, and a menace to peace and organized government.

Grover Cleveland

He mocks the people who proposes that the government shall protect the rich and that they in turn will care for the laboring poor.

Grover Cleveland

I have tried so hard to do right.

Grover Cleveland

I know there is a Supreme Being who rules the affairs of men and whose goodness and mercy have always followed the American people, and I know He will not turn from us now if we humbly and reverently seek His powerful aid.

Grover Cleveland

I would rather the man who presents something for my consideration subject me to a zephyr of truth and a gentle breeze of responsibility rather than blow me down with a curtain of hot wind.

Grover Cleveland

It is better to be defeated standing for a high principle than to run by committing subterfuge.

Grover Cleveland

Minds do not act together in public; they simply stick together; and when their private activities are resumed, they fly apart again.

Grover Cleveland

Officeholders are the agents of the people, not their masters.

Grover Cleveland

Party honesty is party duty, and party courage is party expediency.

Grover Cleveland

Sensible and responsible women do not want to vote. The relative positions to be assumed by man and woman in the working out of our civilization were assigned long ago by a higher intelligence than ours.

Grover Cleveland

Someday I will be better remembered.

Grover Cleveland

Sometimes I wake at night in the White House and rub my eyes and wonder if it is not all a dream.

Grover Cleveland

The lesson should be constantly enforced that though the people support the Government, Government should not support the people.

Grover Cleveland

The ship of Democracy, which has weathered all storms, may sink through the mutiny of those aboard.

Grover Cleveland

The United States is not a nation to which peace is a necessity.

Grover Cleveland

Your every voter, as surely as your chief magistrate, exercises a public trust

Grover Cleveland

I like the noise of democracy.

James Buchanan

The ballot box is the surest arbiter of disputes among free men.

James Buchanan

To avoid entangling alliances has been a maxim of our policy ever since the days of Washington, and its wisdom no one will attempt to dispute.

James Buchanan

The test of leadership is not to put greatness into humanity, but to elicit it, for the greatness is already there.

James Buchanan

What is right and what is practicable are two different things.

James Buchanan

I mean to make myself a man, and if I succeed in that, I shall succeed in everything else.

James Garfield

If wrinkles must be written on our brows, let them not be written upon the heart. The spirit should never grow old.

James Garfield

Territory is but the body of a nation. The people who inhabit its hills and valleys are its soul, its spirit, its life.

James Garfield

Ideas are the great warriors of the world, and a war that has no idea behind it, is simply a brutality.

James Garfield

Nobody but radicals have ever accomplished anything in a great crisis.

James Garfield

Right reason is stronger than force.

James Garfield

A brave man is a man who dares to look the Devil in the face and tell him he is a Devil.

James Garfield

A law is not a law without coercion behind it.

James Garfield

A pound of pluck is worth a ton of luck.

James Garfield

All free governments are managed by the combined wisdom and folly of the people.

James Garfield

Few men in our history have ever obtained the Presidency by planning to obtain it.

James Garfield

He who controls the money supply of a nation controls the nation.

James Garfield

I am trying to do two things: dare to be a radical and not a fool, which is a matter of no small difficulty.

James Garfield

I love to deal with doctrines and events. The contests of men about men I greatly dislike

James Garfield

Ideas control the world.

James Garfield

If the power to do hard work is not a skill, it's the best possible substitute for it

James Garfield

If you are not too large for the place you occupy, you are too small for it.

James Garfield

Justice and goodwill will outlast passion.

James Garfield

Man cannot live by bread alone; he must have peanut butter.

James Garfield

Nine times out of ten the best thing that can happen to a young man is to be tossed overboard and compelled to sink or swim.

James Garfield

Suicide is not a remedy.

James Garfield

The chief duty of government is to keep the peace and stand out of the sunshine of the people.

James Garfield

The civil service can never be placed on a satisfactory basis until it is regulated by law.

James Garfield

The President is the last person in the world to know what the people really want and think.

James Garfield

The truth will set you free, but first it will make you miserable.

James Garfield

Things don't turn up in this world until somebody turns them up.

James Garfield

Whoever controls the volume of money in any country is absolute master of all industry and commerce.

James Garfield

The circulation of confidence is better than the circulation of money.

James Madison

If Tyranny and Oppression come to this land, it will be in the guise of fighting a foreign enemy.

James Madison

A well-instructed people alone can be permanently a free people.

James Madison

As a man is said to have a right to his property, he may be equally said to have a property in his rights.

James Madison

Liberty may be endangered by the abuse of liberty, but also by the abuse of power

James Madison

We are right to take alarm at the first experiment upon our liberties.

James Madison

A pure democracy is a society consisting of a small number of citizens, who assemble and administer the government in person.

James Madison

A well regulated militia, composed of the body of the people, trained in arms, is the best most natural defense of a free country.

James Madison

Each generation should be made to bear the burden of its own wars, instead of carrying them on, at the expense of other generations.

James Madison

No nation could preserve its freedom in the midst of continual warfare.

James Madison

Of all the enemies of public liberty war is, perhaps, the most to be dreaded.

James Madison

The executive has no right, in any case, to decide the question, whether there is or is not cause for declaring war.

James Madison

The means of defense against foreign danger historically have become the instruments of tyranny at home.

James Madison

War contains so much folly, as well as wickedness, that much is to be hoped from the progress of reason.

James Madison

War should only be declared by the authority of the people, whose toils and treasures are to support its burdens, instead of the government which is to reap its fruits.

James Madison

A popular government without popular information or the means of acquiring it, is but a prologue to a farce, or a tragedy, or perhaps both.

James Madison

A man has a property in his opinions and the free communication of them.

James Madison

All men having power ought to be distrusted to a certain degree.

James Madison

Americans have the right and advantage of being armed - unlike the citizens of other countries whose governments are afraid to trust the people with arms.

James Madison

I should not regret a fair and full trial of the entire abolition of capital punishment.

James Madison

If men were angels, no government would be necessary.

James Madison

In Republics, the great danger is, that the majority may not sufficiently respect the rights of the minority.

James Madison

Philosophy is common sense with big words.

James Madison

The essence of Government is power; and power, lodged as it must be in human hands, will ever be liable to abuse.

James Madison

The personal right to acquire property, which is a natural right, gives to property, when acquired, a right to protection, as a social right.

James Madison

A little flattery will support a man through great fatigue.

James Monroe

National honor is the national property of the highest value.

James Monroe

Our country may be likened to a new house. We lack many things, but we possess the most precious of all - liberty!

James Monroe

Preparation for war is a constant stimulus to suspicion and ill will.

James Monroe

It is only when the people become ignorant and corrupt, when they degenerate into a populace, that they are incapable of exercising their sovereignty.

James Monroe

The best form of government is that which is most likely to prevent the greatest sum of evil.

James Monroe

There are two educations. One should teach us how to make a living and the other how to live.

John Adams

Liberty cannot be preserved without general knowledge among the people.

John Adams

Liberty, according to my metaphysics is a self-determining power in an intellectual agent. It implies thought and choice and power.

John Adams

Our Constitution was made only for a moral and religious people. It is wholly inadequate to the government of any other.

John Adams

Power always thinks... that it is doing God's service when it is violating all his laws.

John Adams

Property is surely a right of mankind as real as liberty

John Adams

The essence of a free government consists in an effectual control of rivalries.

John Adams

The right of a nation to kill a tyrant in case of necessity can no more be doubted than to hang a robber, or kill a flea.

John Adams

There is danger from all men. The only maxim of a free government ought to be to trust no man living with power to endanger the public liberty.

John Adams

When people talk of the freedom of writing, speaking or thinking I cannot choose but laugh. No such thing ever existed. No such thing now exists; but I hope it will exist. But it must be hundreds of years after you and I shall write and speak no more.

John Adams

Great is the guilt of an unnecessary war.

John Adams

A government of laws, and not of men.

John Adams

Abuse of words has been the great instrument of sophistry and chicanery, of party, faction, and division of society.

John Adams

Arms in the hands of citizens may be used at individual discretion... in private self-defense.

John Adams

Because power corrupts, society's demands for moral authority and character increase as the importance of the position increases.

John Adams

Remember, democracy never lasts long. It soon wastes, exhausts, and murders itself. There never was a democracy yet that did not commit suicide.

John Adams

Facts are stubborn things; and whatever may be our wishes, our inclinations, or the dictates of our passions, they cannot alter the state of facts and evidence.

John Adams

Fear is the foundation of most governments.

John Adams

I have accepted a seat in the House of Representatives, and thereby have consented to my own ruin, to your ruin, and to the ruin of our children. I give you this warning that you may prepare your mind for your fate.

John Adams

I must study politics and war that my sons may have liberty to study mathematics and philosophy.

John Adams

If we do not lay out ourselves in the service of mankind whom should we serve?

John Adams

My country has contrived for me the most insignificant office that ever the invention of man contrived or his imagination conceived.

John Adams

Old minds are like old horses; you must exercise them if you wish to keep them in working order.

John Adams

Power always thinks it has a great soul and vast views beyond the comprehension of the weak.

John Adams

The Declaration of Independence I always considered as a theatrical show. Jefferson ran away with all the stage effect of that... and all the glory of it.

John Adams

The happiness of society is the end of government.

John Adams

While all other sciences have advanced, that of government is at a standstill - little better understood, little better practiced now than three or four thousand years ago.

John Adams

If your actions inspire others to dream more, learn more, do more and become more, you are a leader.

John Quincy Adams

All men profess honesty as long as they can. To believe all men honest would be folly. To believe none so is something worse.

John Quincy Adams

Nip the shoots of arbitrary power in the bud, is the only maxim which can ever preserve the liberties of any people.

John Quincy Adams

The highest glory of the American Revolution was this: it connected in one indissoluble bond the principles of civil government with the principles of Christianity.

John Quincy Adams

Where annual elections end is where slavery begins.

John Quincy Adams

Always vote for principle, though you may vote alone, and you may cherish the sweetest reflection that your vote is never lost.

John Quincy Adams

America does not go abroad in search of monsters to destroy.

John Quincy Adams

Courage and perseverance have a magical talisman, before which difficulties disappear and obstacles vanish into air.

John Quincy Adams

Popularity, I have always thought, may aptly be compared to a coquette - the more you woo her, the more apt is she to elude your embrace.

John Tyler

I can never consent to being dictated to.

John Tyler

Our country presents on every side the evidences of that continued favor under whose auspices it, has gradually risen from a few feeble and dependent colonies to a prosperous and powerful confederacy.

Martin Van Buren

The people under our system, like the king in a monarchy, never dies

Martin Van Buren

As to the presidency, the two happiest days of my life were those of my entrance upon the office and my surrender of it.

Martin Van Buren

Between Russia and the United States sentiments of good will continue to be mutually cherished.

Martin Van Buren

For myself, therefore, I desire to declare that the principle that will govern me in the high duty to which my country calls me is a strict adherence to the letter and spirit of the Constitution as it was designed by those who framed it.

Martin Van Buren

I tread in the footsteps of illustrious men... in receiving from the people the sacred trust confided to my illustrious predecessor.

Martin Van Buren

If laws acting upon private interests can not always be avoided, they should be confined within the narrowest limits, and left wherever possible to the legislatures of the States.

Martin Van Buren

It seems proper, at all events, that by an early enactment similar to that of other countries the application of public money by an officer of Government to private uses should be made a felony and visited with severe and ignominious punishment.

Martin Van Buren

No evil can result from its inhibition more pernicious than its toleration.

Martin Van Buren

The government should not be guided by Temporary Excitement, but by Sober Second Thought.

Martin Van Buren

The less government interferes with private pursuits, the better for general prosperity.

Martin Van Buren

The national will is the supreme law of the Republic, and on all subjects within the limits of his constitutional powers should be faithfully obeyed by the public servant.

Martin Van Buren

We have reason to renew the expression of our devout gratitude to the Giver of All Good for His benign protection.

Martin Van Buren

It is not strange... to mistake change for progress.

Millard Fillmore

May God save the country, for it is evident that the people will not.

Millard Fillmore

The bold enterprises are the successful ones. Take counsel of hopes rather than of fears to win in this business.

Rutherford B. Hayes

Conscience is the authentic voice of God to you.

Rutherford B. Hayes

Do not let your bachelor ways crystallize so that you can't soften them when you come to have a wife and a family of your own.

Rutherford B. Hayes

Wars will remain while human nature remains. I believe in my soul in cooperation, in arbitration; but the soldier's occupation we cannot say is gone until human nature is gone.

Rutherford B. Hayes

He serves his party best who serves his country best.

Rutherford B. Hayes

I am a radical in thought (and principle) and a conservative in method (and conduct).

Rutherford B. Hayes

I am not liked as a President by the politicians in office, in the press, or in Congress. But I am content to abide the judgment the sober second thought of the people.

Rutherford B. Hayes

One of the tests of the civilization of people is the treatment of its criminals.

Rutherford B. Hayes

The progress of society is mainly the improvement in the condition of the workingmen of the world.

Rutherford B. Hayes

The truth is, this being errand boy to one hundred and fifty thousand people tires me so by night I am ready for bed instead of soirees.

Rutherford B. Hayes

To vote is like the payment of a debt, a duty never to be neglected, if its performance is possible.

Rutherford B. Hayes

Universal suffrage is sound in principle. The radical element is right.

Rutherford B. Hayes

Unjust attacks on public men do them more good than unmerited praise.

Rutherford B. Hayes

The boy who is going to make a great man must not make up his mind merely to overcome a thousand obstacles, but to win in spite of a thousand repulses and defeats.

Theodore Roosevelt

It is only through labor and painful effort, by grim energy and resolute courage, that we move on to better things.

Theodore Roosevelt

The most important single ingredient in the formula of success is knowing how to get along with people.

Theodore Roosevelt

Far and away the best prize that life has to offer is the chance to work hard at work worth doing.

Theodore Roosevelt

Do what you can, with what you have, where you are.

Theodore Roosevelt

In a moment of decision the best thing you can do is the right thing. The worst thing you can do is nothing.

Theodore Roosevelt

The best executive is the one who has sense enough to pick good men to do what he wants done, and self-restraint to keep from meddling with them while they do it.

Theodore Roosevelt

Big jobs usually go to the men who prove their ability to outgrow small ones.

Theodore Roosevelt

People ask the difference between a leader and a boss. The leader works in the open, and the boss in covert. The leader leads, and the boss drives.

Theodore Roosevelt

When you are asked if you can do a job, tell 'em, "Certainly I can!" Then get busy and find out how to do it.

Theodore Roosevelt

Courtesy is as much a mark of a gentleman as courage.

Theodore Roosevelt

If you could kick the person in the pants responsible for most of your trouble, you wouldn't sit for a month.

Theodore Roosevelt

It is hard to fail, but it is worse never to have tried to succeed.

Theodore Roosevelt

I am a part of everything that I have read.

Theodore Roosevelt

Nobody cares how much you know, until they know how much you care.

Theodore Roosevelt

I keep my good health by having a very bad temper, kept under good control.

Theodore Roosevelt

Great thoughts speak only to the thoughtful mind, but great actions speak to all mankind.

Theodore Roosevelt

In life as in a football game, the principle to follow is: Hit the line hard.

Theodore Roosevelt

I am only an average man but, by George, I work harder at it than the average man.

Theodore Roosevelt

Let us remember that, as much has been given us, much will be expected from us, and that true homage comes from the heart as well as from the lips, and shows itself in deeds.

Theodore Roosevelt

The human body has two ends on it: one to create with and one to sit on. Sometimes people get their ends reversed. When this happens they need a kick in the seat of the pants.

Theodore Roosevelt

Nine-tenths of wisdom consists in being wise in time

Theodore Roosevelt

With self-discipline most anything is possible.

Theodore Roosevelt

A good leader can't get too far ahead of his followers.

Theodore Roosevelt

Keep your eyes on the stars, and your feet on the ground.

Theodore Roosevelt

I have only a second rate brain, but I think I have a capacity for action.

Theodore Roosevelt

The only man who never makes a mistake, is the man who never does anything.

Theodore Roosevelt

When angry count to ten before you speak. If very angry, count to one hundred

Thomas Jefferson

Delay is preferable to error.

Thomas Jefferson

It takes time to persuade men to do even what is for their own good.

Thomas Jefferson

Never spend your money before you have earned it.

Thomas Jefferson

Nothing gives one person so much advantage over another as to remain always cool and unruffled under all circumstances.

Thomas Jefferson

Speeches that are measured by the hour will die with the hour.

Thomas Jefferson

The moment a person forms a theory, his imagination sees in every object only the tracts which favor that theory.

Thomas Jefferson

To penetrate and dissipate these clouds of darkness, the general mind must be strengthened by education.

Thomas Jefferson

A coward is much more exposed to quarrels than a man of spirit.

Thomas Jefferson

An injured friend is the bitterest of foes.

Thomas Jefferson

Honesty is the first chapter in the book of wisdom.

Thomas Jefferson

Only aim to do your duty, and mankind will give you credit where you fail.

Thomas Jefferson

The glow of one warm thought is to me worth more than money.

Thomas Jefferson

Educate and inform the whole mass of the people... They are the only sure reliance for the preservation of our liberty.

Thomas Jefferson

I have no fear that the result of our experiment will be that men may be trusted to govern themselves without a master.

Thomas Jefferson

I have sworn upon the alter of God, eternal hostility against every form of tyranny over the mind of man.

Thomas Jefferson

I would rather be exposed to the inconveniences attending too much liberty than those attending too small a degree of it.

Thomas Jefferson

Information is the currency of democracy.

Thomas Jefferson

The boisterous sea of liberty is never without a wave.

Thomas Jefferson

The God who gave us life, gave us liberty at the same time.

Thomas Jefferson

The tree of liberty must be refreshed from time to time with the blood of patriots and tyrants.

Thomas Jefferson

To compel a man to furnish funds for the propagation of ideas he disbelieves and abhors is sinful and tyrannical.

Thomas Jefferson

Whenever the people are well-informed, they can be trusted with their own government.

Thomas Jefferson

An enemy generally says and believes what he wishes.

Thomas Jefferson

As our enemies have found we can reason like men, so now let us show them we can fight like men also.

Thomas Jefferson

Be polite to all, but intimate with few.

Thomas Jefferson

Every citizen should be a soldier. This was the case with the Greeks and Romans, and must be that of every free state.

Thomas Jefferson

For a people who are free, and who mean to remain so, a well-organized and armed militia is their best security.

Thomas Jefferson

I abhor war and view it as the greatest scourge of mankind

Thomas Jefferson

I have seen enough of one war never to wish to see another.

Thomas Jefferson

I think with the Romans, that the general of today should be a soldier tomorrow if necessary.

Thomas Jefferson

It is incumbent on every generation to pay its own debts as it goes. A principle which if acted on would save one-half the wars of the world.

Thomas Jefferson

The most successful war seldom pays for its losses.

Thomas Jefferson

The spirit of this country is totally adverse to a large military force.

Thomas Jefferson

War is an instrument entirely inefficient toward redressing wrong; and multiplies, instead of indemnifying losses.

Thomas Jefferson

We did not raise armies for glory or for conquest.

Thomas Jefferson

A democracy is nothing more than mob rule, where fifty-one percent of the people may take away the rights of the other forty-nine.

Thomas Jefferson

Advertisements contain the only truths to be relied on in a newspaper.

Thomas Jefferson

All tyranny needs to gain a foothold is for people of good conscience to remain silent.

Thomas Jefferson

Always take hold of things by the smooth handle

Thomas Jefferson

Commerce with all nations, alliance with none, should be our motto.

Thomas Jefferson

Conquest is not in our principles. It is inconsistent with our government.

Thomas Jefferson

Determine never to be idle. No person will have occasion to complain of the want of time who never loses any. It is wonderful how much may be done if we are always doing.

Thomas Jefferson

Do not bite at the bait of pleasure, till you know there is no hook beneath it.

Thomas Jefferson

Errors of opinion may be tolerated where reason is left free to combat it.

Thomas Jefferson

Every generation needs a new revolution.

Thomas Jefferson

Every government degenerates when trusted to the rulers of the people alone. The people themselves are its only safe depositories.

Thomas Jefferson

Experience demands that man is the only animal which devours his own kind, for I can apply no milder term to the general prey of the rich on the poor.

Thomas Jefferson

He who knows best knows how little he knows.

Thomas Jefferson

History, in general, only informs us of what bad government is.

Thomas Jefferson

I believe that every human mind feels pleasure in doing good to another.

Thomas Jefferson

I'm a great believer in luck and I find the harder I work, the more I have of it.

Thomas Jefferson

I have no ambition to govern men; it is a painful and thankless office.

Thomas Jefferson

I like the dreams of the future better than the history of the past.

Thomas Jefferson

I never considered a difference of opinion in politics, in religion, in philosophy, as cause for withdrawing from a friend.

Thomas Jefferson

I predict future happiness for Americans if they can prevent the government from wasting the labors of the people under the pretense of taking care of them.

Thomas Jefferson

In matters of style, swim with the current; in matters of principle, stand like a rock.

Thomas Jefferson

It is always better to have no ideas than false ones; to believe nothing, than to believe what is wrong.

Thomas Jefferson

It is error alone which needs the support of government. Truth can stand by itself.

Thomas Jefferson

It is more dangerous that even a guilty person should be punished without the forms of law than that he should escape.

Thomas Jefferson

Money, not morality, is the principle commerce of civilized nations.

Thomas Jefferson

My only fear is that I may live too long. This would be a subject of dread to me.

Thomas Jefferson

My reading of history convinces me that most bad government results from too much government.

Thomas Jefferson

Never put off till tomorrow what you can do today.

Thomas Jefferson

No free man shall ever be debarred the use of arms.

Thomas Jefferson

No government ought to be without censors; and where the press is free no one ever will.

Thomas Jefferson

No man will ever carry out of the Presidency the reputation which carried him into it.

Thomas Jefferson

Nothing can stop the man with the right mental attitude from achieving his goal; nothing on earth can help the man with the wrong mental attitude.

Thomas Jefferson

Nothing is unchangeable but the inherent and unalienable rights of man.

Thomas Jefferson

One travels more usefully when alone, because he reflects more.

Thomas Jefferson

Peace and friendship with all mankind is our wisest policy, and I wish we may be permitted to pursue it.

Thomas Jefferson

Peace, commerce and honest friendship with all nations; entangling alliances with none.

Thomas Jefferson

Politics is such a torment that I advise everyone I love not to mix with it.

Thomas Jefferson

Power is not alluring to pure minds.

Thomas Jefferson

That government is the strongest of which every man feels himself a part.

Thomas Jefferson

The democracy will cease to exist when you take away from those who are willing to work and give to those who would not.

Thomas Jefferson

The second office in the government is honorable and easy; the first is but a splendid misery.

Thomas Jefferson

The strongest reason for the people to retain the right to keep and bear arms is, as a last resort, to protect themselves against tyranny in government.

Thomas Jefferson

There is a natural aristocracy among men. The grounds of this are virtue and talents

Thomas Jefferson

There is not a truth existing which I fear... or would wish unknown to the whole world.

Thomas Jefferson

We never repent of having eaten too little.

Thomas Jefferson

When a man assumes a public trust he should consider himself a public property.

Thomas Jefferson

When we get piled upon one another in large cities, as in Europe, we shall become as corrupt as Europe.

Thomas Jefferson

When you reach the end of your rope, tie a knot in it and hang on.

Thomas Jefferson

Where the press is free and every man able to read, all is safe.

Thomas Jefferson

Labor disgraces no man, but occasionally men disgrace labor.

Ulysses S. Grant

I appreciate the fact, and am proud of it, that the attentions I am receiving are intended more for our country than for me personally.

Ulysses S. Grant

Although a soldier by profession, I have never felt any sort of fondness for war, and I have never advocated it, except as a means of peace.

Ulysses S. Grant

If men make war in slavish obedience to rules, they will fail.

Ulysses S. Grant

If you see the President, tell him from me that whatever happens there will be no turning back.

Ulysses S. Grant

In every battle there comes a time when both sides consider themselves beaten, then he who continues the attack wins.

Ulysses S. Grant

Let us have peace.

Ulysses S. Grant

The art of war is simple enough. Find out where your enemy is. Get at him as soon as you can. Strike him as hard as you can, and keep moving on.

Ulysses S. Grant

There never was a time when, in my opinion, some way could not be found to prevent the drawing of the sword.

Ulysses S. Grant

Hold fast to the Bible. To the influence of this Book we are indebted for all the progress made in true civilization and to this we must look as our guide in the future.

Ulysses S. Grant

I have made it a rule of my life to trust a man long after other people gave him up, but I don't see how I can ever trust any human being again.

Ulysses S. Grant

I know only two tunes: one of them is "Yankee Doodle," and the other isn't.

Ulysses S. Grant

It was my fortune, or misfortune, to be called to the office of Chief Executive without any previous political training.

Ulysses S. Grant

My failures have been errors in judgment, not of intent.

Ulysses S. Grant

Nations, like individuals, are punished for their transgressions.

Ulysses S. Grant

I contend that the strongest of all governments is that which is most free.

William Henry Harrison

There is nothing more corrupting, nothing more destructive of the noblest and finest feelings of our nature, than the exercise of unlimited power.

William Henry Harrison

The chains of military despotism, once fastened upon a nation, ages might pass away before they could be shaken off.

William Henry Harrison

All the measures of the Government are directed to the purpose of making the rich richer and the poor poorer.

William Henry Harrison

The only legitimate right to govern is an express grant of power from the governed.

William Henry Harrison

To Englishmen, life is a topic, not an activity.

William Henry Harrison

In the time of darkest defeat, victory may be nearest.

William McKinley

Expositions are the timekeepers of progress.

William McKinley

That's all a man can hope for during his lifetime - to set an example - and when he is dead, to be an inspiration for history.

William McKinley

War should never be entered upon until every agency of peace has failed.

William McKinley

Our differences are politics. Our agreements are principles.

William McKinley

We need Hawaii just as much and a good deal more than we did California. It is Manifest Destiny.

William McKinley

I have always done my duty. I am ready to die. My only regret is for the friends I leave behind me.

Zachary Taylor

It would be judicious to act with magnanimity towards a prostrate foe

Zachary Taylor